THE LEGACY OF
JOHN PAUL II

JOSEPH CARDINAL RATZINGER

THE LEGACY OF
JOHN PAUL II
IMAGES & MEMORIES

Photographs by
Giancarlo Giuliani

Translated by Michael J. Miller and
Nicoletta V. MacKenzie

IGNATIUS PRESS   SAN FRANCISCO

Original Italian edition: *Giovanni Paolo II: Vent'anni nella storia*
© 1998 by Edizioni San Paolo, s.r.l., Milan

With additions made in 1998
by Joseph Cardinal Ratzinger
as well as his funeral homily
for John Paul II, 2005

Front jacket photograph:
*Pope John Paul II and Joseph Cardinal Ratzinger
greet one another after Pope John Paul's
installation Mass on October 22, 1978*

Jacket photographs by Giancarlo Giuliani/CPP

Jacket design by Roxanne Mei Lum

CONTENTS

"Be Not Afraid", *by Pope John Paul II*   7

John Paul II: Twenty Years in History,
   by Joseph Cardinal Ratzinger   9

The Encyclicals of Pope John Paul II: Milestones
   along the Twenty-Six Years of His Pontificate,
   compiled by Luigi Accattoli   35

Chronology: The Life of Karol Josef Wojtyła,
   compiled by Luigi Accattoli   38

Images of the Pontificate: Twenty Years of the
   Magazine *Famiglia Cristiana* with John Paul II,
   by Leonardo Zega   49

The Pastoral Visits of the Pilgrim Pope throughout
   the World   56

The Later Years   102

Funeral Mass of Pope John Paul II: Homily,
   by Joseph Cardinal Ratzinger   111

"Be Not Afraid"

by Pope John Paul II

When, on October 22, 1978, I said these words in Saint Peter's Square, I could not fully realize how far they would take me and the entire Church. Their meaning came more from the Holy Spirit, the Consoler promised by the Lord Jesus to the apostles, than from the man who spoke them. Nevertheless, with the passing of years, I have recalled these words on many occasions. It was an exhortation to conquer fear in the present world situation, whether in the East or in the West, in the North as well as in the South.

At the end of the second millennium, perhaps we need more than ever these words of the risen Christ: *"Be not afraid!"* Man needs these words because, even after the fall of communism, he has not stopped being afraid and, in reality, has many reasons to feel fear deep within. The peoples and the nations of the entire world need these words. Their consciences need to grow in the certainty that Someone exists who holds in his hands the destiny of this passing world; Someone who holds the keys of death and the netherworld: Someone who is the Alpha and the Omega of human history. And this Someone is Love. Love that became man. Love crucified and risen.

Contemporary man finds it hard to return to faith because he is afraid of the moral demands that faith places before him. The gospel is certainly demanding. If Christ says, *"Be not afraid!"*, he certainly does not say it so as to nullify in some way what he is demanding. God wills man's salvation. He desires the fulfillment of humanity according to the measure he has set. Christ has the right to say that the yoke he places on us is easy and that his burden, when all is said and done, is light. . . . It is very important *to cross the threshold of hope:* not to stop in front of it, but to allow ourselves to be led onward. There is every reason for the truth of the Cross to be called the Good News.

Translated by Nicoletta V. MacKenzie

John Paul II: Twenty Years in History

by Joseph Cardinal Ratzinger

The Ten-Year Pontificate of John Paul II
[Written in 1988]

John Paul II has probably met more people personally than anyone else among our contemporaries. It would be impossible to count the individuals whose hands he has shaken, with whom he has spoken, with whom he has prayed, or whom he has blessed.

Although his office may create distance, his personal radiance creates nearness. Even the simple, the uneducated, and the poor do not have the sense that he is distant, inaccessible, or frightening—feelings that come over one so often in the waiting room of a government official. When you meet this Pope personally, it seems as though the two of you have known each other for a long time, as though you are speaking with a close relative or a good friend. The title "Father" appears not to be a title at all but rather the expression of a real relationship that you experience in his presence.

Everyone knows John Paul II: his face, his characteristic way of moving and of speaking; his immersion in prayer and his spontaneous cheerfulness.

Translated from German by Michael J. Miller.

Page 6: Karol Wojtyła, immediately after being elected Pope on October 16, 1978.
Page 8: John Paul II signing the apostolic constitution that promulgated the new Code of Canon Law (January 25, 1983). At his side stands Cardinal Joseph Ratzinger.
Pages 10–11: The Pope's daily routine.
Page 13: The Pontiff during a meeting with the cardinals in charge of the Pontifical Congregations (above) and with Cardinal Joseph Ratzinger (below).

But anyone who studies the papal and personal writings of Pope John Paul II can easily recognize that this Pope knows very well how to distinguish between the entirely personal works of Karol Wojtyła and his official doctrinal pronouncements as Pope. The reader will also recognize that these are not two completely separate things; rather, they are one personality that is informed by the faith of the Church. His "I", his personality, has been placed entirely at the service of the "We". He has not drawn the "We" down into the subjective realm of private opinions; rather, he has clothed it with a personality that is thoroughly informed by this "We" and stands for it.

I believe that this fusion of "We" and "I", which has matured in his life of faith and his reflection upon it, is the essential reason for what is fascinating about this papal figure. It allows him to move about quite freely and matter-of-factly in this office; it allows him to be thoroughly himself as Pope, without having to fear that he is thereby pulling the office down too much into the subjective sphere.

But how did this inner unity develop? How does a personal path of believing, thinking, and living lead so completely into the center of the Church? This is a question that goes far beyond mere biographical curiosity. For precisely this "identification" with the Church, without any hypocrisy or schizophrenia, seems impossible today to so many people who are struggling to keep the faith.

In contemporary theology, meanwhile, it has become the almost flirtatious fashion to maintain a critical distance from the faith of the Church and to let the reader sense that the author is not so naïve or uncritical or submissive as to place his intellectual work entirely in the service of this faith. This approach does indeed devalue the faith, without increasing the value of the hasty outlines drawn up by the theologians, which become obsolete as quickly as they are brought forth. Thus today there is a reawakening of a great longing for honest intellectual thinking about the faith so that it can be lived anew.

"The vocation of Karol Wojtyła matured as he was working in a chemical factory during the horrors of war and occupation"

The vocation of Karol Wojtyła matured as he was working in a chemical factory during the horrors of war and occupation. He himself described the experience that he gained during four years in a working-class milieu as the decisive developmental phase of his life. It was there that he did his philosophical studies, poring over books filled with abstractions that at first appeared to him like an impassable jungle. His point of departure had been philology, the love of language, combined with the artistic application of language as a representation of reality in a new form of theater. Thus matured the particular kind of "philosophy" that is characteristic of the present Pope. It is thought in confrontation with the concrete; it consists of thinking on the basis of the great tradition, but with a view to corroborating it in the present. It is thought that proceeds from artistic observation, a kind of thinking with

pastoral insight: oriented toward the human person so as to show him the way.

I think that it is interesting to inquire into the series of influential authors that Wojtyła encountered. The first one, as he relates in his conversations with André Frossard, was a textbook introduction to metaphysics. Whereas other students try to grasp to some extent the intrinsic logic of the conceptual terminology presented and to commit it to memory in preparation for their exams, he began to wrestle with the subject in order to gain a real understanding of it, that is, to relate the concept with the experience. And in fact after two months of struggling, the "lightning bolt" struck: "I discovered what a deep meaning was concealed in all that I had previously only lived and suspected."

Then came his encounter with Max Scheler and, thus, with "phenomenology". This philosophical approach intends, after the endless debate about the limits and possibilities of human knowledge, simply to look again at the phenomena, as they appear to us, in their variety and richness. This precise way of seeing, this understanding of man, not by means of abstractions and principles, but rather through a loving comprehension of his reality, became and remains a crucial element in the Pope's thinking.

Finally, he discovered early on, even before his vocation to the priesthood, the works of Saint John of the Cross, through which the interior world "of the soul that has matured in grace" opened up to him.

The metaphysical, the mystical, the phenomenological, and the aesthetic—the interplay of all these aspects opened his eyes to the many levels of reality and finally became a single comprehensive perception [*Wahrnehmung*] that confronts everything that appears and manages to understand it through the fact that the perception goes beyond it. The crisis of postconciliar theology is to a large extent a crisis of its philosophical foundations. The philosophy handed down in the schools of theology lacked a fullness of perception; it lacked phenomenology, and it lacked the mystical dimension. But when the philosophical foundations are not clearly explained, theology loses its footing. For then it is no longer clear to what extent man perceives reality at all or what foundations can serve as the basis for his thought and discourse. Thus it seems to me to be a providential arrangement that at this time a "philosopher" has ascended to the Chair of Peter, a philosopher who carries on philosophy, not as a textbook science, but rather as the product of the struggle for existence in reality, as a consequence of the encounter with the searching, questioning human person.

"The way for the Church is man"

The theme of Karol Wojtyła's philosophy was and is man. His pastoral vocation had an ever greater impact on his academic interest in the subject. Against this background it is understandable that collaborating on the conciliar Constitution on the Church in the Modern World (a text that is centered on a concern for man) was an important experience for the future Pope. "The way for the Church is man." This statement, which is quite

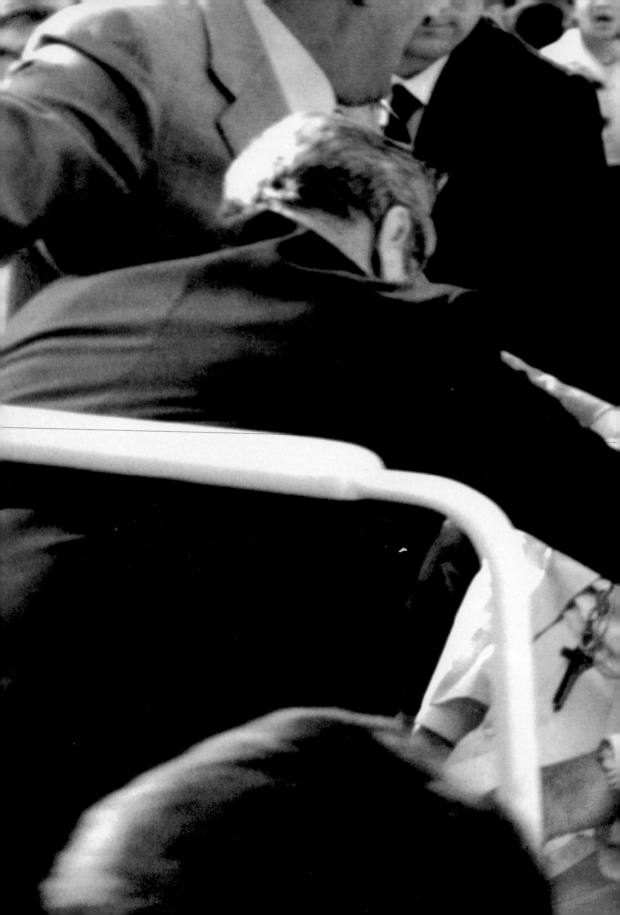

concrete yet radically profound and suggestive, is the central idea in a body of thought that is simultaneously action. Given this point of departure, it followed logically that the question of moral theology became central to his theological work.

That, too, was a significant personal advantage for someone who was to hold the office of Supreme Pastor in the Church. For the crisis of philosophical orientation has its most pronounced effects in the crisis of moral theological instruction. Here the connection between philosophy and theology, between rational inquiry into man and the theological enterprise, is so obvious as to be unavoidable. When the old metaphysics falls apart, the Commandments also lose their inner coherence; then there is a great temptation to set them aside as an artifact of cultural history.

> *"When the old metaphysics falls apart, the Commandments also lose their inner coherence"*

Wojtyła had learned from Scheler how to investigate, with unprecedented human empathy, the nature of virginity, marriage, motherhood and fatherhood, the language of the body, and, thus, the essence of love. He incorporated the new findings of personalism into his thought, but in so doing he came to understand again that the body itself speaks, that creation speaks and gives us instruction. Modern philosophy opened up a new dimension for moral theology, and Wojtyła made use of it in the interplay between reflection and experience, between his pastoral and his intellectual vocation, and understood this new dimension in union with the perennial themes of tradition.

Something else was important for this existential and intellectual path, for this unity of experience, thought, and faith. After all, this man's struggle did not play itself out in a more or less private circle, simply within the precincts of a factory or of a seminary. It was surrounded by the signs of the times, the great, burning issues of history. The fact that Wojtyła worked in the factory was connected with the arrest of his university professors. His peaceful academic career had been interrupted and replaced by the terribly difficult apprenticeship of life among an oppressed people. Affiliation with the clandestine seminary of Cardinal Sapieha was per se an act of resistance. Thus the question about freedom, about human dignity and human rights, about the political responsibility of the faith, was not introduced into the young theologian's thought as a theoretical problem. It was the extremely real and concrete affliction of his hour. Meanwhile the particular situation of Poland at the point of intersection between East and West had once more become that country's destiny.

From critics of the Pope one often hears the remark that he, being a Pole, knows nothing but the sentimental, traditional piety of his country and hence cannot completely understand the complicated issues of the Western world. There is nothing more foolish than such a remark, which shows a complete ignorance of history. One has only to read the encyclical *Slavorum apostoli* in order to get some idea of how it was precisely his Polish heritage that compelled the Pope to think in terms of a plurality of cultures. Because Poland is the point of intersection of various cultures, standing in the midst of Germanic, Romance, Slavic, and Greco-Byzantine traditions, the issue of dialogue with separated Christians and dialogue with different cultures is in many respects more urgent there than elsewhere. And so precisely this Pope is a genuinely ecumenical and truly missionary Pope, who in this regard was providentially prepared for the issues of the period following the Second Vatican Council.

"The issue of dialogue with separated Christians and dialogue with different cultures is in many respects more urgent there than elsewhere"

Let us return once more to the pastoral and anthropological concern of the Pope. "The way for the Church is man." The true meaning of this much-misunderstood sentence from the encyclical *The Redeemer of Man* becomes evident only when we recall that, for the Pope, "man" in the fullest sense is Jesus Christ. There is nothing of that self-sufficient anthropocentrism in his passion for man. Anthropocentrism is opened up to a higher perspective. That form of anthropocentrism which tried to exclude God as a competitor to man has long since turned into a loathing for man. Man is no longer fond of regarding himself as the center of the world; he is afraid of his own destructive power.

"That form of anthropocentrism which tried to exclude God as a competitor to man has long since turned into a loathing for man"

Wherever man is moved to center stage at God's expense, it disturbs the entire equilibrium; then the saying from the Letter to the Romans applies, which says that the world has been caught up into the groaning and travail of man (Rom 8:22); trampled down by Adam, it now awaits the appearance of the sons of God and its liberation (Rom 8:19, 21). Because the Pope is concerned about man, he would like to open wide the doors to Christ. For only through Christ's entrance can the children of Adam become children of God and liberty be restored to both man and creation. The Pope's anthropocentrism, therefore, is most profoundly theocentrism.

Although his first encyclical seemed to concentrate entirely on man, his three great theological encyclicals automatically combined to form one trinitarian triptych. With this Pope, anthropocentrism *is* theocentrism, because he lives out his pastoral vocation on the basis of prayer, and his experience with man is undertaken in fellowship with God, from whom he has learned to understand it.

We should add one more thing. Certainly his profound love for Mary is in the first place the heritage of his Polish homeland. But his encyclical about Mary demonstrates that this Marian devotion has a biblical basis and has been thoroughly worked out through prayer and lived experience. Just as his philosophy became concrete and alive through phenomenology, through contemplation of reality as it appears, so too this Pope's relationship to

Christ does not stop at the abstract level of the great dogmatic truths; rather it is a concrete human encounter with the Lord in his full reality and, thus, necessarily an encounter with his Mother, in whom the Israel of faith, the praying Church, has become a person. And then again it is true that one's relationship with the Lord acquires its warmth and vitality only from this concrete proximity, which sees the mystery of Christ in all the richness of its divine and human fullness. And, of course, the fact that the faith-response took shape perpetually in a woman, in Mary, has a retroactive effect on our whole concept of man.

What do I mean to say by all that? My object in these remarks has been to demonstrate the unity of office and person in the figure of Pope John Paul II. He really has "identified" himself with the Church, and that is why he can also be her voice. All this is not said in order to praise a man. It is said in order to show that faith does not extinguish thought and does not have to bracket off the experience of our time. On the contrary: only faith gives breadth to thought and meaning to experience. Man becomes free, not by becoming a soloist, but rather by finding the relationship in which he belongs.

The Twenty-Year Pontificate of John Paul II
[Written in 1998]

A book on the Pope *again*? Is that necessary? Has not everything already been said? Is it not just repeating over and over what we already know? The casual observer might think that the second decade in the pontificate of Pope John Paul II could not possibly bring much more that is new after the great spiritual awakening [*Aufbruch*] of the first decade. Yet anyone who looks even a little more closely will recognize that this pontificate continues to have surprises in store and that the later years, too, are marked by a very special sort of fruitfulness and have features that are quite distinctive.

Of course, the initial enthusiasm about this youthful, energetic Pope, his openness to all the issues of this time, his love for life, his willingness to try what is unusual and to break out of customary arrangements and formalities—that is gone. There were times of bitter criticism; here and there it seemed that sheer lack of interest in the words of this tireless, globe-trotting pilgrim had prevailed. But then, after all, astonished ears would prick up once more, and again and again would come a word, a gesture, that brushed away the annoyance and touched the heart.

"Astonished ears would prick up once more, and again and again would come a word, a gesture, that brushed away the annoyance and touched the heart"

It happened this way on many of his trips in recent years. It had been announced that the old man was no longer of interest to anybody and that his message was completely outdated. But, lo and behold, when he arrived, the power of his personality was stronger than

any snap judgments that had been formulated. I am thinking, for example, of his recent visit to France [in September 1996]. The occasion was quite delicate. The commemoration of the baptism of Clovis I [in A.D. 496], which was supposed to be celebrated as the beginning of the history of France, had unexpectedly launched the French into a vehement debate about their past. To associate the beginning of France with Clovis seemed to many to be a clerical usurpation of that history, which was glorious precisely because it had to be read from the perspective of a "lay", that is, secular hermeneutic.

Within the Church, too, the question necessarily arose whether it was right to let the Pope step into the middle of the seething cauldron of this dispute, in which he would be bound to present particular scenes from history, perhaps one-sidedly. But once he was there, the quarrel was swept aside. He spoke so simply from the midst of the faith experience and addressed so directly the questions that concern us in this hour of world history that those present were united in a great celebration of the faith and outsiders were led into a new reflectiveness. During that same visit the Pope, who is made out to be a strict moralist and the messenger of a severity that ignores human needs, found words full of understanding for people on the margins of society and at the perimeter of the Church, for the foundering and the suffering and the questioning, for the discouraged and the helpless, so as to spread confidence and at the same time to develop a willingness to tolerate and accept one another, which is the true core of Christian morality.

At this point we should mention a very important characteristic of the recent years in the pontificate of Pope John Paul II. The man who spoke to the crowds in this way was himself suffering. Pain has been imprinted on his face. He is bent over; he walks with difficulty and now uses the shepherd's staff that ends in a cross and symbolizes his papal ministry as a cane on which he leans. He leans on the cross, on the Crucified. One might expect that, as a result, his attractiveness to young people, which had become more evident with each passing year, would now be over and done with. What could a sick, suffering, tired old man, who in moments of exhaustion has obvious difficulty in speaking, possibly have to say to them?

"The man who spoke to the crowds in this way was himself suffering. Pain has been imprinted on his face"

"He leans on the cross, on the Crucified"

This concern had been particularly worrisome in the weeks leading up to the [August 1997] World Youth Day in Paris. Many newspapers were already reporting as a foregone conclusion that the numbers in attendance would be extremely disappointing. But the huge crowds that poured into the city so far surpassed even the optimistic estimates that it caused a considerable problem for the organizers of the event. And although the heat, too, did its best to make the encounter unmanageable, it ended up being for all who participated an unforgettable time of joy, during which the young people finally began to sense what life is, what life could and should be.

I have been able to speak about these days with many of the participants, including some who had gone to the event with great skepticism. But I have not met a single one who was not carried away by the atmosphere of this encounter in faith. Suddenly it was a beautiful thing again to be a Christian. The young pilgrims discovered that it is wonderful to pray together, to be silent together, to receive the Sacrament of Penance and thus to be reconciled with oneself, with God, and with others; that it is a beautiful thing to celebrate Eucharist and to experience in it the Lord's presence.

Of course many factors contributed to the success of the event; I believe that we simply cannot overlook the healing power of the presence of the living God. But absolutely essential for these days was, no doubt, the fact that in the Pope the reality of the Church became tangible—the reality of the mystery that surpasses human ability and human expertise. One could say that the suffering Pope was in a special way transparent to the presence of Someone Greater. He was standing in the center, and yet it was not exactly he, that man, who stood in their midst, but rather Christ, for whom he "stands in" as a substitute.

"In the Pope the reality of the Church became tangible—the reality of the mystery that surpasses human ability and human expertise"

On that occasion I suddenly understood the Pauline expression "I boast of my weakness" in a completely new way. The Apostle means to say that he himself, with his gifts and strengths, is simply unequal to the great responsibility that he has assumed. But precisely for this reason it became clear that he was not building something for himself, that ultimately he was not the one who established the Church of the Gentiles; instead, the power came from somewhere else altogether.

The same thing struck me again at the Eucharistic Congress in Bologna. The Pope seemed tired and was stressed. And then came the rock stars for the young people, Bob Dylan, or whatever their names were. They had an entirely different message from the one for which the Pope stood. One might be skeptical—I was, and in a certain sense I still am—as to whether it was right to let that band of "prophets" make an appearance there. But how outmoded and meager their message suddenly appeared to be when the Pope put his manuscript aside and simply spoke from the heart to those young people and said things to them that might seem too demanding, at least to start with: about the meaning of failure, of renunciation, of accepting suffering and the cross.

This was not a presentation of shopworn, empty religious formulas; someone was speaking there who—as the rite of priestly ordination puts it—had placed "his life under the sign of the cross" and by doing so had become wise.

And the listeners were touched by something that is completely overlooked in all that the travel and entertainment industries have to offer and in the modern way of spending one's life: something that nevertheless

concerns each one of us personally. For somewhere in all of that there is an inadequacy; it does not challenge me to do my best and my utmost, and somehow everyone still knows that.

It seems to me that a special message of this second half of his pontificate can be found precisely in this physical and spiritual suffering of the Pope. Today everything is geared to results and efficiency. The politician has to radiate youthful vigor, so that he appears electable; modern managerial jobs require a high degree of physical performance. Strangely enough, in a society that is noticeably becoming older, the cult of youth continues to thrive. Sickness and suffering must be concealed as far as possible. The Pope does not conceal it; he cannot and will not conceal it. By that very fact he renders us an important service. Old age, too, has its message; suffering has its dignity and its healing power.

"Old age, too, has its message; suffering has its dignity and its healing power"

I will never forget how the Pope, during the solemn Mass for the Synod of African Bishops, which he had been looking forward to so much, spoke to us from the hospital after having fallen in the bathroom and broken his right hip. He had previously visited the shrine of Our Lady of Tears in Syracuse [Sicily], and he spoke to us about this encounter. No sermon he might have addressed to us in good health could have touched us in a similar fashion. Our Lady of Tears stood for all the tears of the innocent people whom no one comforts. How many tears have been shed in this decade in Africa—whether we think of Rwanda, Mozambique, Nigeria, Guinea-Bissau, or of so many other countries. The suffering Pope spoke on behalf of the suffering in this world and had entered in a completely unforeseen way, with a moving reality, into the sufferings of Africa, and so he was also an authentic messenger of Divine Mercy, the trustworthy voice admonishing human beings to practice mercy.

During the second decade of his pontificate, however, the Pope has also produced magisterial works of extraordinary density and intensity, which in comparison with his first few encyclicals have very distinctive features. The encyclical letters from the early years bear the strong imprint of the Pope's personal reflections and meditations; the great trinitarian triptych, *Redemptor hominis—Dives in misericordia—Dominum et vivificantem* [entitled in English: "The Redeemer of Man"—"The Mercy of God"—"The Holy Spirit in the Life of the Church and the World"], shows the unmistakable handwriting of the Pope. The train of his thought is quite perceptible in the magisterial documents from his second decade as well. It charts the course and sets the tone. Yet these are far-reaching magisterial documents, which, on the one hand, carefully address the current status of a given question and, on the other hand, confront it with tradition as a whole and hence teach us how continuity and development are to be combined.

In this regard I am thinking especially of the great encyclical on the foundations of moral theology (*Veritatis splendor*), which can safely be called an epoch-making document, a milestone in the elaboration of the moral message of Christianity, which goes far beyond the circle of believers to speak to the conscience of all men. I am thinking also of the missionary encyclical *Redemptoris missio*, which considers anew the missionary duty of the Church within the context of today's dialogue among religions and defines the correct relation between dialogue and proclamation. Then there is *Evangelium vitae*, a hymn to life, as it were, within the context of an anti-culture of death, in which an inordinate and sickened desire for life makes death its helpmate and reinvents the business of killing, in abortion and euthanasia, as though it were a boon for mankind.

> *"I am thinking especially of the great encyclical on the foundations of moral theology (Veritatis splendor), which can safely be called an epoch-making document"*

These texts occasionally met with a more positive reception among thinkers outside the Church than among some exponents of Catholic theology. This is particularly true of the magisterial document about the fundamental questions of moral theology. Many non-Christian thinkers perhaps feel the heat of mankind's moral crisis more intensely than many theologians; they sense that the destruction of moral consciousness threatens humanity more than atomic energy and diseases. Or rather: the atom bomb and the injustice in the world that produces ever-increasing hunger and misery threaten us only because moral shortcomings have led to this misuse of human knowledge and human power and will continue to exacerbate it unless something decisive happens to oppose it.

In his encyclical the Pope developed a vision of morality that, on the one hand, is large and broad enough to include the moral wisdom of the great religious traditions and of human reason. The appeal to reason, to its ability to perceive the order of the Creator in creation, is a fundamental aspect of this text. On the other hand, however, the document sets forth that new certainty and that new concreteness of morality which came into the world through Christ and which becomes a force for mankind as a whole whenever believers live it in such a way that it is made evident to others as well. The publication of another magisterial document has been announced for the autumn of this year [1998]; in it the question of faith and reason, which remains in the background in *Veritatis splendor*, is supposed to be the main theme, and therefore it will address the topics of the public responsibility and the communicability of the faith. We are anxiously awaiting this document [*Fides et ratio*, published on September 14, 1998].

> *"Fides et ratio will address the topics of the public responsibility and the communicability of the faith"*

I would like to mention also a second series of papal documents of this past decade. Already in his first encyclical, which was published shortly after the beginning of his pontificate, the Pope had referred to the approach of the year 2000 and had spoken frankly of an Advent season of the Church: she has come a long way, yet she does not look back; rather, she looks forward. Together with Christ, who has come, she walks to meet the Lord, who is to come. As the Pope sees it, this millennial occasion [*Datum*] for remembering the Incarnation is by its very nature an occasion for hope. Christ lives; he is able and he wants to renew the world in the midst of all its crises, so that it becomes open to the kingdom of God.

Looking ahead to the year 2000 was and is for the Pope the same as looking to the living power of the Risen One, to the One who accomplishes more than we are capable of. But it is also a challenge to go forth to meet him. Three important documents from recent years have now been coordinated with this thought. First there is the ecumenical encyclical letter *Ut unum sint*: from the very beginning the Pope has increasingly experienced the division of Christianity as a wound that affects him quite personally— that actually causes physical pain. He regards it as his duty to do everything he can to reach a turning point toward unity. And so he has put all his ecumenical passion into this document; in places it sounds almost like a cry in distress for help, so that he may become a servant of unity and so that the third millennium may take shape, after the divisions of the second, as a time of coming together again.

"He may become a servant of unity and so that the third millennium may take shape ... as a time of coming together again"

Besides this great encyclical there is another ecumenical magisterial document by the Pope that has remained too much in the shadows: the apostolic letter *Orientale lumen*, into which the Slavic Pope has put all his love for the Churches of the East. "A Pope, son of a Slav people, is particularly moved by the call of those peoples to whom the two saintly brothers Cyril and Methodius went. They were a glorious example of apostles of unity who were able to proclaim Christ in their search for communion between East and West amid the difficulties that [even then] sometimes set the two worlds against each other", we read in paragraph 3. This papal letter constitutes a precious little summa of Eastern Christian spirituality, a doctrinal work that could bring the heritage of the East into our Western mind-set [*Geistigkeit*], which tends toward rationalism, and thus bring us closer together again on the basis of the interior fulfillment of the spiritual life.

Finally, I would like to refer to the apostolic letter *Tertio millennio adveniente*, which pertains directly to the Jubilee Year 2000. In it the Pope not only provides a sober yet magnificent interpretation of this celebration, but he also develops a thoroughly practical pastoral program for its preparation and execution. One could say that this letter is a little handbook for the new evangelization, which is such a concern of the Holy Father. The idea of penance and the idea of joy interpenetrate here in a surprising way. And although the theme of God predominates, elaborated in the trinitarian faith of the Church in the Father, the Son, and the Holy Spirit, this fundamental theme of all of human life is interwoven in a very practical way with the attitudes of faith, hope, and love, as well as with the sacraments of Baptism, Confirmation, Penance, and Holy Eucharist. Thus a spiritual ecclesiology appears, in which everything refers to God, in which God himself has become our way through the sacraments of the living Church.

Today even critical minds are becoming more clearly aware of the fact that the crisis of our time consists of the "crisis of God", the disappearance of God from the horizon of human history. Thus the Church's response can only be to speak less and less about herself and more and more about God, to witness to him, to be a doorway for him.

And doing this is the real program of the pontificate of John Paul II, which with the passing of years only becomes more and more apparent. So let this short attempt at an appreciation conclude with the Aaronic blessing, which the liturgical renewal has selected as a reading for the beginning of the year, on New Year's Day, which has become the feast day of the Mother of God, who is so profoundly honored and loved by John Paul II:

> May the LORD bless him and keep him:
> May the LORD make his face to shine upon him,
>   and be gracious to him:
> May the LORD lift up his countenance upon him,
>   and give him peace.
>
> (cf. Num 6:24–26)

Captions for photos on pp. 17–34

Page 17: The Pope during a brief summer vacation in Lorenzago di Cadore, Italy. – *Pages 18–19*: A dramatic moment captured on film immediately after the assassination attempt on May 13, 1981 (photo courtesy of Olympia-Ansa). – *Page 23*: May 1988: the affectionate embrace of a Bolivian boy in Tarija. – *Page 25*: John Paul II on Monte Chetif in the Valle d'Aosta, September 7, 1986. – *Page 27*: At Tours, France, during a celebration of the Eucharist in September 1996 (photo courtesy of Olympia-Reuters). – *Page 29*: John Paul II in prayer on the Hill of the Crosses, a symbol of the martyrdom suffered by Lithuanian Catholics at the hands of the Soviets, during his trip to the Baltic countries in September 1993. – *Page 31*: The Pope working at his desk in his private apartments. – *Page 34*: The opening of the Holy Door on the occasion of the Jubilee Year, March 25, 1983.

THE ENCYCLICALS OF JOHN PAUL II
Milestones along the Twenty-Six Years of His Pontificate

Redemptor hominis *(March 4, 1979)*, on Christ, "the Redeemer of man". This is the first encyclical of his pontificate, and it announces its program.

Dives in misericordia *(November 30, 1980)*, on the fatherhood of God, who is "rich in mercy".

Laborem exercens *(September 14, 1981)*, on man who earns his daily bread by "doing work", that is, about human work.

Slavorum apostoli *(June 2, 1985)*, on Eastern Christianity and on the heritage of the "Apostles of the Slavs", Saints Cyril and Methodius.

Dominum et vivificantem *(May 18, 1986)*, about the Holy Spirit, "the Lord and giver of life". (Together with **Redemptor hominis** and **Dives in misericordia**, this encyclical completes a trilogy on the Trinity.)

Redemptoris Mater *(March 25, 1987)*, on Marian devotion, which is given to "the Mother of the Redeemer".

Sollicitudo rei socialis *(December 30, 1987)*, on the "social concern" of the Church.

Redemptoris missio *(December 7, 1990)*, on the missionary activity of the Church, which originates in "the mission of the Redeemer".

Centesimus annus *(May 1, 1991)*, on the social question, in observance of the one hundredth anniversary of **Rerum novarum**. (This encyclical, **Laborem exercens**, and **Sollicitudo rei socialis** form a trilogy dedicated to Catholic social doctrine.)

Veritatis splendor *(August 6, 1993)*, on the foundations of morality, which must be guided by "the splendor of truth".

Evangelium vitae *(March 25, 1995)*, on abortion, euthanasia, and the death penalty, to urge humanity, at the conclusion of the millennium, to react against the culture of death with "the Gospel of Life".

Ut unum sint *(May 25, 1995)*, on ecumenism, in response to Christ's prayer "that they may be one". It invites other Christian Churches and ecclesial communities to "seek together" new ways of exercising papal primacy so that it can be accepted by everyone.

Fides et ratio *(September 14, 1998)*, on the relationship between "faith and reason" in contemporary thought.

Ecclesia de Eucharistia *(April 17, 2003)*, on the Eucharist and its relationship to the Church.

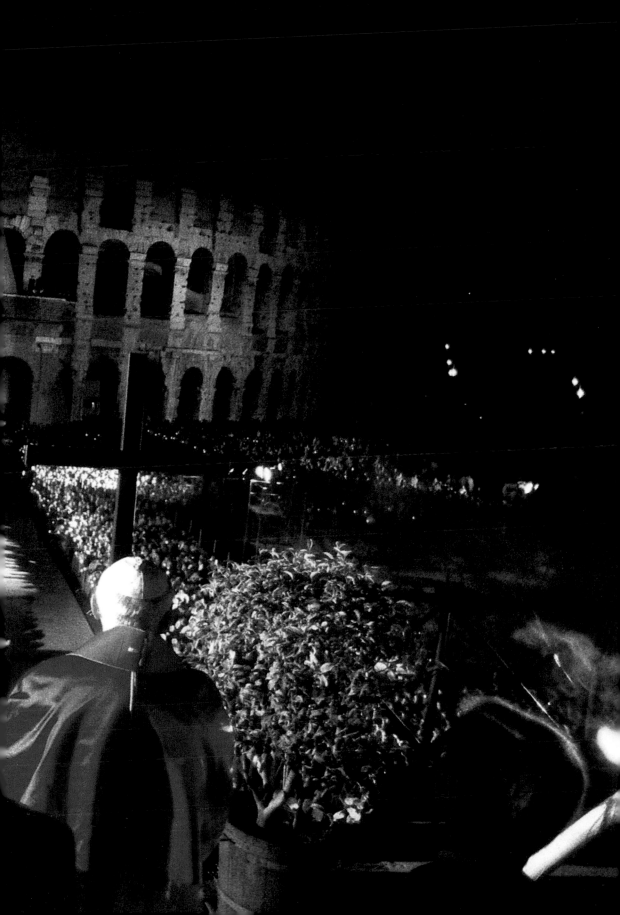

CHRONOLOGY
The Life of Karol Josef Wojtyła

1920   *May 18*: Karol Jósef Wojtyła is born in Wadowice to Karol Wojtyła and Emilia Kaczorowska.

1929   *April 13*: His mother, Emilia Kaczorowska, dies.

1932   His eldest brother Edmund, a doctor, dies.

1938   In August he moves to Kraków and enrolls in the Faculty of Literature.

1941   *February 18*: His father dies of a heart attack. Karol is left with no family. In March, he begins working as a laborer in the stone quarries of Zakrzówek. With his friend Mieczysław Kotlarczyk he founds the Rhapsodic Theater of Kraków.

1942   In October he begins to attend clandestine classes of the Faculty of Theology of the Jagellonian University. He is transferred from the quarry to the Solvay chemical plant.

1944   *February 29*: He is hit by a military truck and hospitalized. In August, he enters the clandestine seminary founded by Archbishop Sapieha in his own residence.

1946   *November 1*: He is ordained a priest and travels to Rome to continue his studies.

1948   *June 14*: Obtains a doctorate degree in Rome with his thesis on *The Problems of Faith in the Works of Saint John of the Cross* and returns to Poland. He is appointed assistant pastor in Niegowić, near Gdów, then in Kraków, in the parish of Saint Florian.

1953   *December 1*: Accredited to teach at the Jagellonian University after defending a thesis on Max Scheler.

1956   *December 1*: Appointed to the Chair of Ethics at the Catholic University of Lublin, a position he will hold until his election as Pope.

1958   *July 4*: Becomes Auxiliary Bishop of Kraków.

1962   In October, goes to Rome to attend the Second Vatican Council.

1964   *January 13*: Appointed Archbishop of Kraków.

1967   *June 28*: Is consecrated Cardinal.

1969   *February 28*: Visits the Kazimierz Synagogue in Kraków.

1971   *October 5*: Is elected to the Council of the Secretary General of the Synod of Bishops; goes on to be reelected in 1974 and 1977.

1972   *May 8*: Convenes the Synod of the Archdiocese of Kraków. Publishes the book *Foundations of Renewal: A Study on the Implementation of the Second Vatican Council*.

1974   *September 27–October 26*: Serves as *relator* at the Synod of Bishops on evangelization.

1976   Preaches the Lenten retreat at the Vatican in March.

1978   *October 16*: Elected Pope with the name of John Paul II.

1979   *November 10*: Announces the "reexamination" of the Galileo case.

1980   *September 26–October 25*: Convokes the Synod of Bishops on "The Role of the Christian Family in the Modern World". *December 30*: Proclaims Saints Cyril and Methodius (together with Saint Benedict) Patrons of Europe in his apostolic letter *Egregiae Virtutis*.

1981   *May 13*: Victim of an assassination attempt in Saint Peter's Square, he is admitted twice to the Gemelli Polyclinic. Finally leaves the hospital on August 14. *November 25*: Nominates Cardinal Joseph Ratzinger as Prefect of the Congregation for the Doctrine of the Faith.

(continued on page 42)

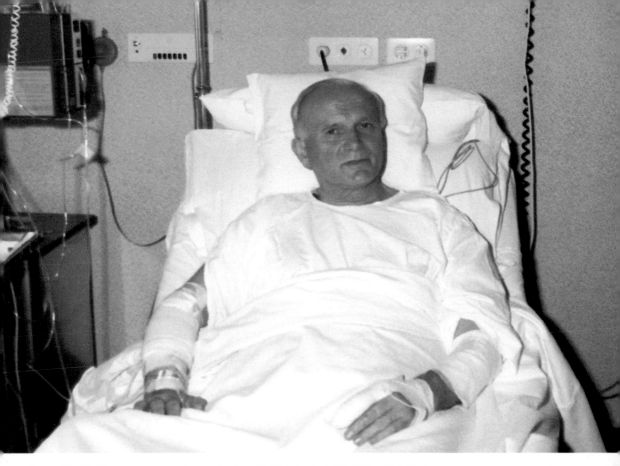

Pages 36–37: Every year, on the evening of Good Friday, the Pope leads the ceremony of the Way of the Cross in the impressive setting of the Colosseum.
Page 39: The Pope as a patient in the Gemelli Polyclinic after the attempt on his life (above); his meeting with his would-be assassin, Alì Agca, in Rebibbia Prison (below) (photo by A. Mari, *L'Osservatore Romano*).
Pages 40–41: Assisi, World Day of Prayer for Peace, with representatives of all world religions, on October 27, 1986.
Page 43: Meeting with Mother Teresa of Calcutta, February 3, 1986.
Pages 44–45: The historic visit of John Paul II to the synagogue in Rome, April 13, 1986.
Page 47: Millions cheer Pope John Paul II during his first papal visit to his native Poland in 1979 (above); Pope John Paul II and President Ronald Reagan, 1987 (below).
Page 48: The Pope embraces Cardinal Wyszyński during the ceremony inaugurating his pontificate.

(continued from page 38)

1983   *January 25*: Promulgates the new Code of Canon Law. *March 25*: Inaugurates the Holy Year of Redemption. *September 29–October 29*: Convokes the Synod of Bishops on "Penance and Reconciliation in the Mission of the Church". *December 27*: Meets his would-be assassin, Mehmet Alì Agca, in Rebibbia Prison.

1985   *March 31*: Publishes the apostolic letter *Dilecti amici*, to the Youth of the World on the occasion of the United Nation's International Youth Year.

1986   *April 13*: Visits the synagogue in Rome. *October 27*: Presides in Assisi over the first World Day of Prayer for Peace, along with representatives of world religions.

1987   *June 6*: Inaugurates the Marian Year in Saint Peter's Square. *October 1–30*: Convokes the Synod of Bishops on "The Vocation and Mission of the Lay Faithful in the Church and in the World". *December 3–7*: Receives at the Vatican a visit from the Ecumenical Patriarch of Constantinople, Dimitrios I.

1988   *July 2*: Ratifies the excommunication of the schismatic followers of traditionalist Bishop Marcel Lefèbvre. *September 30*: Publishes the apostolic letter *Mulieris dignitatem*, on the dignity and vocation of women.

1989   *January 30*: With the post-synodal exhortation *Christifideles laici*, he invites bishops to appreciate ecclesial movements. *December 1*: Receives Mikhail Gorbachev, who invites him to visit the U.S.S.R.

1990   *September 30–October 28*: Convokes the Synod of Bishops on "The Formation of Priests".

1991   *January 15*: Writes to Saddam Hussein and George Bush, on the expiration date of the United Nations' ultimatum, in an attempt to prevent the Gulf War.

1992   *July 12–July 28*: Is admitted to the Gemelli Polyclinic for the removal of a colon tumor. *October 11*: Apostolic constitution *Fidei depositum*, on the publication of the new *Catechism of the Catholic Church*. *October 31*: The "reexamination" of the Galileo Case concludes with the "honest acknowledgment" of the wrongs done to the scientist.

1993   *January 9–10*: Along with Christians, Jews, and Muslims, participates in the "Day of Fasting and Prayer" in Assisi for peace in the Balkans. *November 11*: Following a fall in the *Sala delle Benedizioni* [Hall of Blessings at the Vatican], he is hospitalized for the fourth time.

1994   *April 29–May 27*: Hospitalized for the fifth time for a hip replacement, following a fall in the bathroom. *June 13–14*: Calls an extraordinary consistory to prepare for the Great Jubilee. *October 2–29*: Holds a synod of bishops on consecrated life. *October 20*: Publishes *Crossing the Threshold of Hope*, a book based on an interview with Vittorio Messori. *November 14*: Publishes the apostolic letter *Tertio millennio adveniente*, in preparation for the Great Jubilee, in which he proposes to reexamine the "dark pages" in the history of the Church.

1995   *July 10*: Publishes the *Letter to Women* during the International Year of the Woman.

1996   *February 22*: Promulgates the apostolic constitution *Universi dominici gregis*, reforming the rules for a conclave. *October 6–15*: Hospitalized, once again, for an appendectomy. *November 15*: Publishes the autobiographical book *Gift and Mystery: On the Fiftieth Anniversary of My Priestly Ordination*.

1998   *March 12*: Issues a letter to accompany the report *We Remember: A Reflection on the Shoah*, published by the Commission on Catholic-Jewish Relations. *October 15*: Publishes encyclical letter *Fides et ratio*, on the relationship between faith and reason. *October 16*: Celebrates the twentieth anniversary of his pontificate.

(continued on page 46)

46

(*continued from page 42*)

1999 *October 1*: In a *Motu proprio* proclaims Saints Bridget of Sweden, Catherine of Siena, and Teresa Benedicta of the Cross Co-Patronesses of Europe. *December 24*: Opens the Holy Door in Saint Peter's Basilica and proclaims the Great Jubilee of the Year 2000.

2000 *March 12*: Presides at Mass and a prayer service in Saint Peter's Basilica on the "Day of Pardon" of the Holy Year 2000, in which the Church prays for forgiveness for the historical sins of her children. *April 30*: In the first canonization of the Jubilee Year, declares Sister Maria Faustina Kowalska (1905–1938), of the Sisters of the Blessed Virgin Mary of Mercy, a Saint. *May 13*: Beatifies Francesco and Jacinta Marto and announces that the "third part" of the secret of Fatima will be made public. *June 26*: The Message of Fatima is published in its entirety. *August 15–20*: Two million attend the fifteenth World Youth Day in Rome on the Campus of Tor Vergata. *September 3*: Beatifies Popes Pius IX and John XXIII.

2001 *January 6*: Closes Holy Door in Saint Peter's Basilica to end Holy Year 2000 and signs the apostolic letter *Novo millennio ineunte*. *August 1*: Gives his one thousandth General Audience. *November 18*: After the terrorist attacks of September 11, 2001, and during the war in Afghanistan, asks Catholics to celebrate a day of fasting for peace (December 14, 2001).

2002 *January 24*: At Assisi, participates in a Day of Prayer for Peace in the World with members of other Churches and ecclesial communities and with representatives of other religions. *February 11*: Creates an ecclesiastical province in Russia and elevates four apostolic administrations in that country to the rank of diocese. *October 16*: On the twenty-fifth anniversary of his pontificate, signs the apostolic letter *Rosarium Virginis Mariae* to mark the beginning of the Year of the Rosary; introduces the new Mysteries of Light.

2003 *June 5–9*: Makes his one hundredth Apostolic Visit outside Italy: a five-day visit to Croatia. *October 16*: Celebrates a Mass of Thanksgiving on Saint Peter's Square on the twenty-fifth anniversary of his pontificate. *October 19*: Beatifies Mother Teresa of Calcutta.

2004 *June 10*: Proclaims Year of the Eucharist, scheduled to begin with the Eucharistic Congress in Guadalajara, Mexico (October 10–17, 2004), and to end with the Synod of Bishops on the Eucharist in Rome (October 2–29, 2005). *June 29*: Receives Ecumenical Patriarch Bartholomew I of Constantinople to mark fortieth anniversary of the meeting of Paul VI and Athenagoras I in Jerusalem in January 1964. *November 27*: Presents to Patriarch Bartholomew I in Saint Peter's Basilica part of the relics of Saints John Chrysostom and Gregory Nazianzen as a gift to the Orthodox Church of Constantinople.

2005 *February 1–10*: Hospitalized at the Gemelli Polyclinic with respiratory ailments. *February 24*: Again hospitalized at the same clinic; leaves by motorcade on March 13 to return to the Vatican. *March 25*: Participates in the Stations of the Cross at the Colosseum on Good Friday from his private chapel via closed-circuit television. *March 27*: Imparts his blessing to the crowds on Saint Peter's Square on Easter Sunday after his message *Urbi et orbi* is read by Cardinal Sodano. *March 30*: Condition worsens. *April 2*: After First Vespers of Divine Mercy Sunday (the Second Sunday of Easter), dies peacefully at 9:37 P.M. while crowds pray the Rosary on Saint Peter's Square. *April 4–7*: Lies in state in Saint Peter's Basilica while millions of pilgrims from all over the world pay their last respects. *April 8*: Funeral Mass on Saint Peter's Square and burial in the crypt of Saint Peter's Basilica.

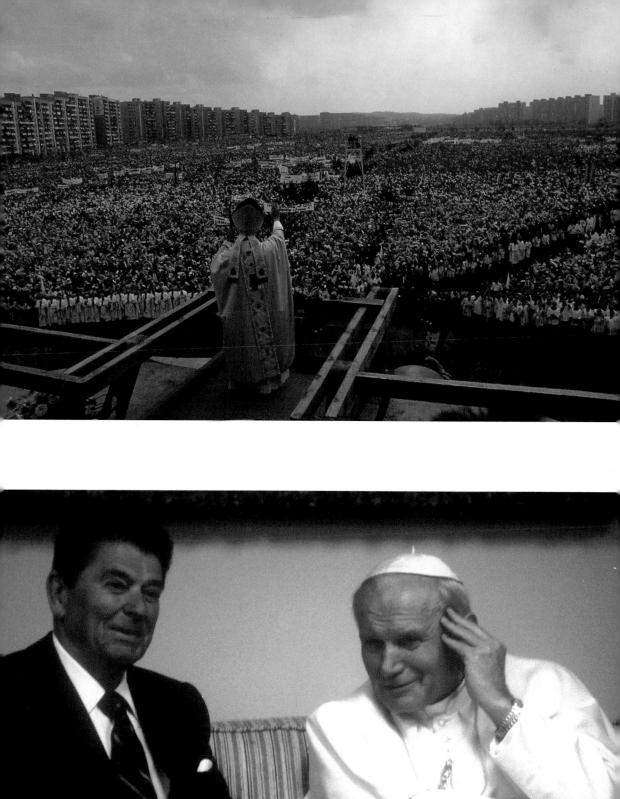

IMAGES OF THE PONTIFICATE

Twenty Years of the Magazine Famiglia Cristiana
with John Paul II

by Leonardo Zega

A t 7:00 P.M. on October 16, 1978, when it was announced that the new Pope was the Cardinal of Kraków and that his name was Karol Wojtyła, many people in Italy asked themselves in amazement, "Wojtyła? Who in the world is that?!" It was not just "the man in the street" who asked himself that question. On the evening of the election, there was panic in Corso Sempione, at the Milan headquarters of RAI, the Italian national television and radio network, two steps away from the editorial offices of *Famiglia Cristiana*. They had little information and only a few old photos. How could they put together a decent documentary on the life of this Pope who "comes from afar"?

They called us, asking whether we could give them a hand. Of course we would help. On June 21 of the same year—four months before becoming Pope—Karol Wojtyła had been with us to give an opening address of great doctrinal depth to the international congress on "Fruitful and Responsible Love", which had been organized by the Center for Family Education (the cultural arm of the magazine *Famiglia Cristiana*), in observance of the tenth anniversary of the encyclical *Humanae vitae*.

A few had turned up their noses when we decided to invite him. To discourage us, they told us: No one knows him; he is not a great theologian; we have better speakers of our own here. However, to those who were responsible for the congress and those who had been called in as advisors—theologians, scholars, social workers, international experts in family matters—Karol Wojtyła was far from being an "unknown". Because of his prestige and education, he was just the right

Translated by Nicoletta V. MacKenzie.

Cardinal Karol Wojtyła during his address at the CISF *Famiglia Cristiana* Congress, marking the tenth anniversary of *Humanae vitae* (1978).

person to speak on that topic to such a highly qualified audience.

His keynote lecture met with unanimous approval, and his encounter with about four hundred delegates from fifty-seven different countries immediately revealed the personality of the Cardinal of Kraków: solid, simple, tremendously human. (That evening, during dinner, he "slipped away" after the soup to watch the semi-finals of the soccer world cup, which were being broadcast from Argentina.) The Italian press, even the Catholic newspapers and magazines, did not devote much space to the congress and minimized the Cardinal's address. They made up for it later on, when the "unknown" Cardinal unexpectedly ascended to the Chair of Saint Peter, and they all asked us whether they could reprint that speech, which, all of a sudden, had become "important".

50

This is how we, at *Famiglia Cristiana*, came into contact with John Paul II during that momentous "year of the three popes", as 1978 has been called. In a commemorative booklet that was published after his election to the papacy, we can still read today both the text of the lecture given by the then Cardinal and also the testimonies of some of the participants who visited with him before and after his speech. I will quote the reactions of two particularly noteworthy witnesses.

The first is from a Protestant theologian who at the time was in charge of the Family Office of the Ecumenical Council of Churches, Ma Mpolo Masamba, from the Congo.

The man who today has become the spiritual head of the Roman Catholic Church spent some ten minutes with me, reviewing a panorama of family topics that are of interest to our Churches. This conversation and his opening address revealed to me certain characteristics of Cardinal Karol Wojtyła that I might sum up in this way: he is a man with an open mind toward other Churches, which are made up, not only of "separated brethren", but of Christians who bring different spiritual dimensions to Christianity. A man full of sympathy and warmth toward persons of different cultures and races. A man whose approach is characterized by a sense of conciliatory dialogue, who is ready to serve as an intermediary between individuals and countries whose systems of thought and whose political and economic visions are, at times, in conflict. A man who grew up in a Church guided by tradition but who is free because he believes in the reforming power of the Divine Spirit. His commentary on *Humanae vitae* was couched, not in philosophical or biological terms, but in the language of a pastor who shares in the joy and the anguish of the human couple. He reminded the couples of the divine character of fruitful love without ulterior motives, a love that is never exhausted and that transmits life, not only because it brings new lives into existence, but also because it creates fruitful interaction between two persons, in a relationship that has been sanctified indissolubly.

The second testimony is from Professor Gustave Martelet, a member of the International Theological Commission.

With John Paul II, the Church of silence and poverty now has her turn to speak and

(*continued on p. 53*)

takes the helm so as to serve Christ in the Church of Peter. Thus, humanly speaking, the boat of the fisherman is handed over, for the second time, to a son of laborers. Furthermore, it is being handed over today for the first time to a son of a Church that has recently been despoiled of her temporal goods and thus has become an eminently "evangelical" Church. Who can maintain that today, especially in the West, we have no need of trembling once more in holy fear while listening to this new voice that calls us to greatness and to our Christian duties?

And further on he writes:

As far as I am concerned, it is clear that if we had guessed that Cardinal Wojtyła would be the next Pope, I would never have dared to take the microphone before he did at that congress. Everyone would have prevented me from doing so. Everyone, that is, except him. One thing is certain: his ministry as Pope in Rome will be marked by the same character as his lecture in Milan when he was a cardinal: an absolute fidelity to the [Second Vatican] Council, in its entirety.

Two years later, in November 1980, he received me in a private audience with my closest associates to mark the fiftieth anniversary of *Famiglia Cristiana*. Our meeting extended well beyond the time allotted by the protocol and enabled us to appreciate John Paul II's interest in and respect for the communications media, which he, "the great communicator" (as he has been called), immediately learned to use with the intelligence of a world leader and the authority of a universal Pastor. During our audience, he recalled the Congress of Milan, and especially Father Zilli, whom he had met on March 31 of that same year, on the very morning of his unexpected death. Among other things, he told us: "Remember the great responsibility you have to spread the faith. You have a large parish, a great apostolate. Your founder, Father Alberione, had this charism. I think that, in an image-oriented society such as we live in today, it is very, very important to reach many people through the medium of the press." From that day, *Famiglia Cristiana* has never let go of the Pope, and not just because of our duty as a news journal. We have reported on all of his actions. We have

published and offered to our readers the complete text of his encyclicals and of most of the documents of his pontificate. We have followed him on his trips throughout the world, as the photographs in this book testify. They were taken by our journalist and photographer Giancarlo Giuliani, who was also able to capture some personal and private moments of John Paul II, thanks to his familiarity with the Vatican precincts.

Reviewing these past twenty years of history, in which John Paul II has held a central position, with one of his closest collaborators, Cardinal Joseph Ratzinger, as our guide and accompanied by photographs that capture for us the highlights of his ministry is not just like thumbing through a family album. It is reflecting on the meaning of a pontificate, the longest of this [twentieth] century, and on the providential destiny of this Pope, who, without giving in to fatigue and suffering, interprets literally Christ's mandate: "Go therefore and make disciples of all nations" (Mt 28:19).

We would like to remind all of our families, especially, of the great love and constant care that John Paul II has always shown for them. One quotation should suffice, taken from a speech that he gave in Nairobi, Kenya, on June 7, 1980:

> The Christian family is also the domestic sanctuary of the Church. In a Christian family we rediscover different aspects of the Church in her totality, such as mutual love, listening to the Word of God, and common prayer. The home is the place where the gospel is received and lived out and from which it then radiates. Furthermore, the family offers a daily, sometimes silent witness to the truth and the grace of the Word of God.

Pages 50–51: The crowd participates in the Mass celebrated on the banks of the Congo River, at Kisangani (Zaire), May 6, 1980.
Page 52: The affectionate welcome in the Favela dos Alagados in Salvador da Bahia, Brazil, July 7, 1980.
Page 53: John Paul II in San Francisco, September 18, 1987.
Pages 54–55, 57: The Pope disembarking from an airplane, during one of his many trips.

THE PASTORAL VISITS OF
THE PILGRIM POPE
THROUGHOUT THE WORLD

1979

Dominican Republic, Mexico, the Bahamas: January 25–February 1.

Poland: June 2–10.

Ireland and U.S.: September 29–October 8.

Turkey: November 28–30.

1980

Zaire, Congo, Kenya, Ghana, Upper Volta (Burkina Faso), Côte d'Ivoire (Ivory Coast): May 2–12.

France: May 30–June 2.

Brazil: June 30–July 12.

Federal Republic of Germany: November 15–19.

1981

Pakistan, Philippines, Guam (U.S.), Japan, Anchorage (U.S.): February 16–27.

1982

Nigeria, Benin, Gabon, Equatorial Guinea: February 12–19.

Portugal: May 12–15.

Great Britain: May 28–June 2.

Argentina and Rio de Janeiro (Brazil, II: second visit): June 10–13.

Geneva (Switzerland): June 15.

San Marino: August 29.

Spain: October 31–November 9.

1983

Lisbon (Portugal II), Costa Rica, Nicaragua, Panama, El Salvador, Guatemala, Honduras, Belize, Haiti: March 2–10.

Poland (II): June 16–23.

Lourdes (France II): August 14–15.

Austria: September 10–13.

1984

Fairbanks (U.S.), Republic of Korea, Papua New Guinea, Solomon Islands, Thailand: May 2–12.

Switzerland (II): June 12–17.

Canada: September 9–21.

Spain (II), Dominican Republic, San Juan (Puerto Rico): October 10–13.

1985

Venezuela, Ecuador, Peru, Trinidad and Tobago: January 26–February 6.

The Netherlands, Luxembourg, Belgium: May 11–21.

Togo, Côte d'Ivoire (II), Cameroon, Central African Republic, Zaire (II), Kenya (II), Morocco: August 8–19.

Kloten (Switzerland III), Liechtenstein: September 8.

1986

India: January 31–February 11.

Colombia and Saint Lucia: July 1–8.

France (III): October 4–7.

Bangladesh, Singapore, Fiji, New Zealand, Australia, Seychelles: November 18–December 1.

1987

Uruguay, Chile, Argentina (II): March 31–April 13.

Federal Republic of Germany (II): April 30–May 4.

Poland (III): June 8–14.

U.S. (II), Fort Simpson (Canada II): September 10–21.

(continued on page 58)

58

(*continued from page 56*)

1988

Uruguay (II), Bolivia, Lima (Peru II),
  Paraguay: May 7–19.
Austria (II Trip): June 23–27.
Zimbabwe, Botswana, Lesotho, Swaziland,
  Mozambique: September 10–19.
France (IV): October 8–11.

1989

Madagascar, La Réunion, Zambia,
  Malawi: April 28–May 6.
Norway, Iceland, Finland, Denmark,
  Sweden: June 1–10.
Santiago de Compostela, Asturias (Spain
  III): August 19–21.
Seoul (Republic of Korea II), Indonesia
  (East Timor), Mauritius: October 6–16.

1990

Cape Verde, Guinea-Bissau, Mali, Burkina
  Faso (II), Chad: January 25–February 1.
Czechoslowakia: April 21–22.
Mexico (II), Curaçao: May 6–14.
Malta: May 25–27.
Tanzania, Burundi, Rwanda, Yamous-
  soukro (Côte d'Ivoire III): September
  1–10.

1991

Portugal (III): May 10–13.
Poland (IV): June 1–9.
Czestochowa (Poland V), Hungary:
  August 13–20.
Brazil (III): October 12–21.

1992

Senegal, Gambia, Guinea: February 19–26.
Angola, São Tomé and Principe:
  June 4–10.
Dominican Republic (III): October 9–14.

1993

Benin (II), Uganda, Khartoum (Sudan):
  February 3–10.
Albania: April 25.
Spain (IV): June 12–17.
Jamaica, Mérida (Mexico III), U.S. (III):
  August 9–16.
Lithuania, Latvia, Estonia: September
  4–10.

1994

Zagreb (Croatia): September 10–11.

1995

Manila (Philippines II), Port Moresby
  (Papua New Guinea II), Sydney
  (Australia II), Colombo (Sri Lanka):
  January 11–21.
Czech Republic (II), Poland (VI):
  May 20–22.
Belgium (II): June 3–4.
Slovakia (II): June 30–July 3.
Yaoundé (Cameroon II), Johannesburg-
  Pretoria (Republic of South Africa),
  Nairobi (Kenya III): September 14–20.
Newark, New York, United Nations
  Organization, Yonkers, Baltimore (U.S.
  IV): October 4–9.

1996

Guatemala (II), Nicaragua (II), El Salva-
  dor (II), Venezuela (II): February 5–12.
Tunisia: April 14.
Slovenia: May 17–19.
Germany (II): June 21–23.
Hungary (II): September 6–7.
France (V): September 19–22.

1997

Sarajevo (Bosnia and Herzegovina): April
  12–13.
Czech Republic (III): April 25–27.
Beirut (Lebanon): May 10–11.
Poland (VII): May 31–June 10.
Paris (France VI): August 21–24.
Rio de Janeiro (Brazil III): October 2–6.

(*continued on page 102*)

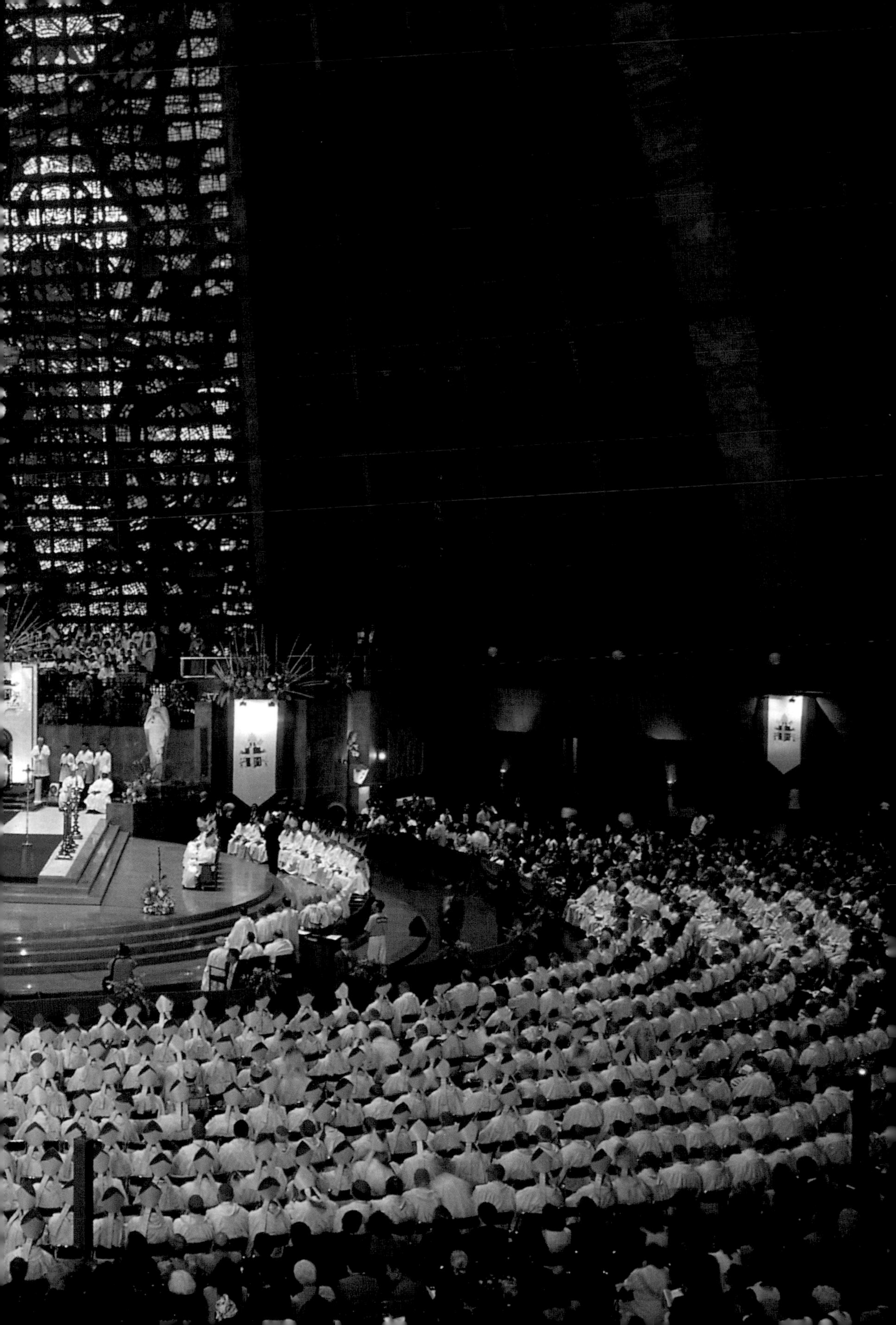

Page 59: In an address to the United Nations General Assembly in New York, October 5, 1995, Pope John Paul II calls himself "a witness to human dignity, a witness to hope, a witness to the conviction that the destiny of all nations lies in the hands of a merciful Providence".

Pages 60–61: The Mass celebrated by John Paul II in the Metropolitan Cathedral of Rio de Janeiro during his visit to the Brazilian city, October 2–6, 1997.

Page 62: A scene from his first visit to Poland, June 2–10, 1979.

Page 63: Among John Paul II's first trips, especially memorable were the ones to Mexico (above) in January 1979 and to Turkey (lower right), from November 28 to 30 of the same year.

Page 64: In May 1984, the Pope took a long trip that brought him to the United States, then to the Pacific Islands, and from there as far as Korea and Thailand. The photo (above) shows a moment from his trip to New Guinea. In 1987, Pope John Paul II enjoying the snow and mountain air during a vacation in the northern Italian village of Lorenzago di Cadore, in the Dolomites (lower left).

Page 65: On June 15, 1984, during his visit to Switzerland, John Paul II celebrated Mass in the Benedictine Abbey of Einsiedeln (above). During his trip to Canada in September 1984, he met with Huron women and children inside a tent (below).

Pages 66–67: Meeting with King Hassan II of Morocco in Casablanca, August 19, 1985.

Page 68: Meeting with representatives of the European Community in Luxembourg, during his visit to Benelux from May 11 to 21, 1985 (above), and a moment of prayer during his trip to Zimbabwe in 1988 (below).

Page 69: The Pope comes out of an Indian tent that was set up for a eucharistic liturgy during his visit to Canada in 1987.

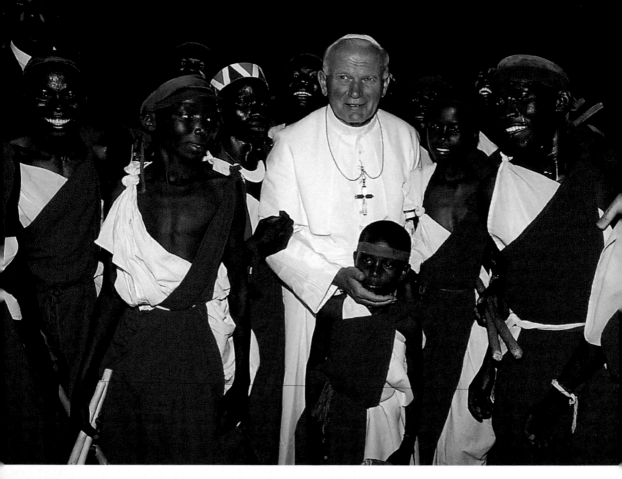

Page 70–71: Pope John Paul II accepts a hard hat from a workman in Oruru, Bolivia during a pastoral visit there in May, 1988.

Pages 72–73: A tremendous crowd gathered in Seoul to greet the Pope during his visit to Korea in October 1989.

Page 74: The Pope in Bujumbura, among some faithful wearing traditional Burundian costumes, during his trip of September 1990 (above). A snapshot of the impressive performance given in honor of the Pontiff during his visit to Mexico in May 1990 (below).

Page 75: John Paul II, pilgrim at Santiago de Compostela, August 1989.

Page 76: In prayer at the tomb of Cardinal Mindszenty, during his trip to Hungary in August 1991 (above left). The meeting with Sister Lucia dos Santos, at Fatima, during his trip to Portugal in May of the same year (above right). Welcome by Polish President Lech Wałęsa at the Koszalin airport during the Pope's trip to Poland in June 1991 (below).

Page 77: John Paul II with thurible in hand incensing the statue of Our Lady of Fatima, during his trip to Portugal in May 1991.

Page 78: The Pope surrounded by the faithful in the Shrine of Popooguine, during his trip to Senegal, in February 1992.

Page 79: John Paul II in the door of the House of Slaves, on the Senegalese island of Gorée.

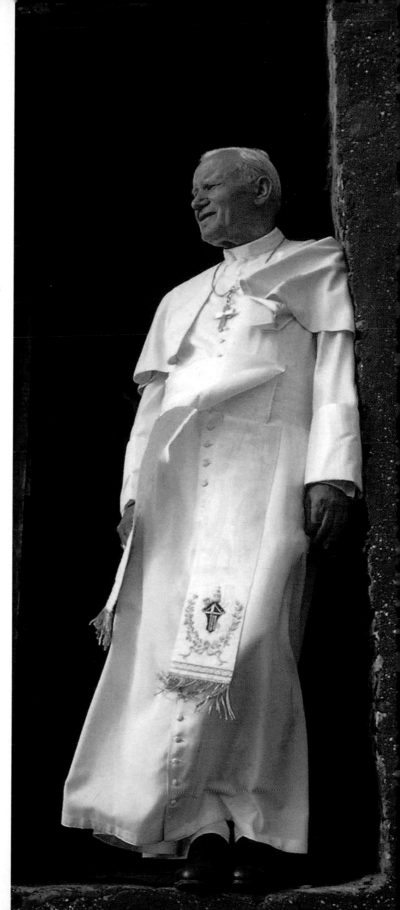

Page 80: The Pontiff blessing the crowds while leaving the Shrine of the Nativity in Siluva, Lithuania, during his trip to the Baltic countries in September 1993.

Page 81: John Paul II watches as a group of women dance in his honor, at the airport in Kasese, Uganda, during his trip to Africa in February 1993 (above). Aerial view of Green Square, in Khartoum, during the Mass celebrated by John Paul II (below).

Pages 82–83: Aerial view of the Mass celebrated by John Paul II in the Plaza de Colon, Madrid, on the occasion of his trip to Spain in June 1993.

Pages 84: A display of affection toward an African child, on his arrival at Antananarivo, during his trip to Madagascar in 1989.

Page 85: John Paul II during a meeting with leaders of other religions in Colombo, during his trip to Sri Lanka in January 1995 (above). Among the lepers of Cumura, in Guinea-Bissau, during his trip to Africa in January 1990 (below).

Page 86: The Pope holds the hands of two young Czechs during a meeting in Olomuc in 1995 (above). The Sri Lanka Armed Forces salute the Holy Father during his visit in January 1995 (below).

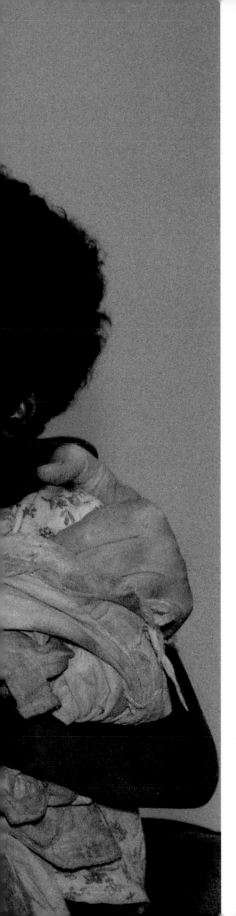

Page 88: John Paul II receives gifts from two young Slovaks dressed in traditional garb, 1995 (above). During his trip to Central America in February 1996, John Paul II pays a courtesy visit to the Guatemalan President, Alvaro Arzú. In the photograph, he blesses a baby in its mother's arms (below).

Page 89: A scene before the Mass celebrated in Maribor, Slovenia, in May 1996 (above). The Pope in an airplane with Cardinal Ratzinger, on his third journey to Germany in June 1996 (below).

Pages 90–91: The Olympic Stadium in Berlin, filled with the faithful during the Mass for the beatification of Bernhard Lichtenberg and Karl Leisner, celebrated by John Paul II during his trip to Germany in June 1996.

Page 92: John Paul II, German Chancellor Helmut Kohl, and Bishop Karl Lehmann in Berlin, in front of the Brandenburg Gate, the final stop in his visit to Germany in June 1996.

Page 93: The meeting between the Pontiff and Dom Helder Camara in the Cathedral of Rio de Janeiro during his trip to Brazil, October 2–6, 1997 (above). The celebration of the six hundredth anniversary of the Faculty of Theology of the Jagellonian University in Kraków, which was observed during his trip to Poland in 1997 (below).

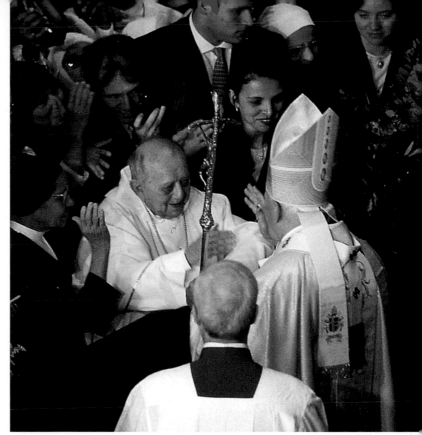

Page 94: John Paul II in the basilica of Notre Dame in Paris on August 22, 1997.
Page 95: The historic encounter with Cuban President Fidel Castro during John Paul II's visit to the Caribbean island in January 1998.
Pages 96–97: The Pope greets fourteen thousand boy scouts gathered in Piani di Pezza (L'Aquila, Italy) on August 9, 1986.

Page 98: John Paul II addressing young people at World Youth Day in Rome, August, 2000.
Page 99: Pilgrims fill St. Peter's Square during the Jubilee Year in Rome, 2000–2001 (above). Celebration of Holy Easter, St. Peter's Square, 2000 (below).

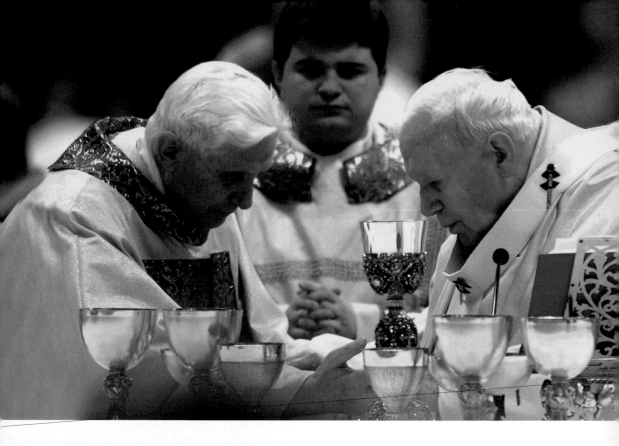

Page 100: Pope John Paul II and Cardinal Joseph Ratzinger celebrating Mass together (above). Pope John Paul II at the Holy Door, St. Peter's Basilica, January 6, 2001 (below).
Page 101: Pope John Paul II opens the international eucharistic congress. Vatican, June 18, 2000.

(continued from page 58)

1998
Cuba: January 21–26.
Nigeria: March 21–23.
Austria: June 19–21.
Croatia (II): October 2–4.

1999
Mexico (IV), St. Louis (U.S. V): January
  22–28.
Romania: May 7–9.
Poland (VII): June 5–17.
Slovenia (II): September 19.
New Delhi (India II), Georgia: November
  5–9.

2000
Mount Sinai, Egypt: February 24–26.
The Holy Land (Jordan, Autonomous
  Palestinian Territories, Israel): March
  20–26.
Fatima (Portugal IV): May 12–13.

2001
Greece, Syria, Malta: May 4–9.
Ukraine: June 23–27.
Kazakhstan, Armenia: September 22–27.

2002
Azerbaijan, Bulgaria: May 22–26.
Toronto (Canada III), Guatemala City
  (Guatemala III), Mexico City
  (Mexico V): July 23–August 2.
Kraków (Poland VIII): August 16–19.

2003
Spain (V): May 3–4.
Croatia (III): June 5–9.
Bosnia and Herzegovina: June 22.
Slovak Republic (III): September 11–14.

2004
Bern (Switzerland IV): June 5–6.
Lourdes (France VII): August 14–15.

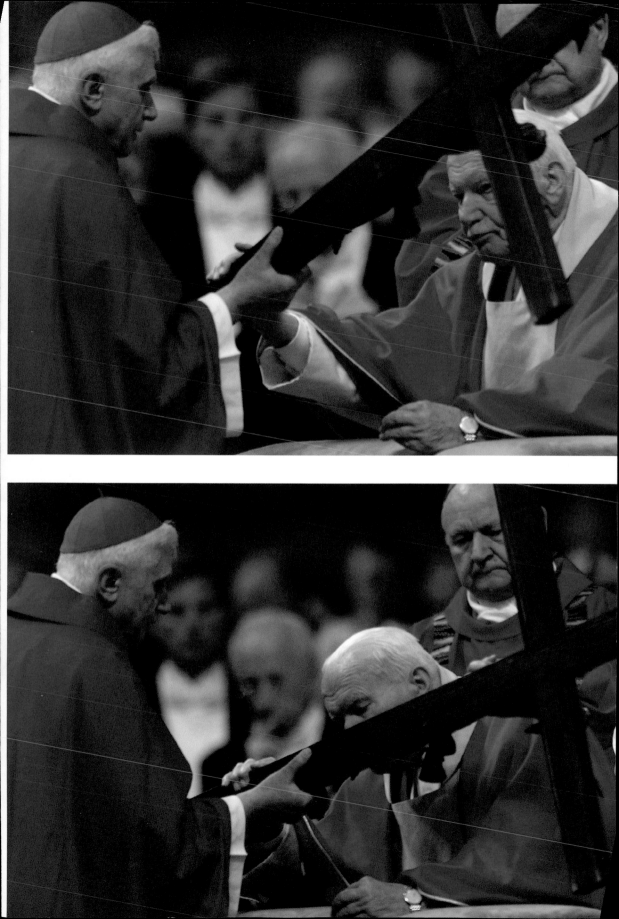

Page 102: Pope John Paul II celebrates Mass at Korazim, The Mount of Beatitudes, during his trip to the Holy Land. March 24, 2000.

Page 103: Pope John Paul II arrives on Mount Nebo where, according to tradition, it was from here that Moses saw the Promised Land after leading the Israelites through the desert for forty years. Amman, Jordan, March 20, 2000.

Page 104: Pope John Paul elevates the Blessed Sacrament as he leads Mass in Loreto, northern Italy, September 5, 2004. (Photo by Alessia Giuliani)

Page 105: Pope John Paul II venerates a cross held by Cardinal Joseph Ratzinger during the Good Friday liturgy at the Colosseum in Rome, April 9, 2004 (above and below).

Page 106–107: Pope John Paul II appears at the window of his private apartments for the last time on Easter Sunday, March 27, 2005. Anguished and unable to speak, he gives his Easter blessing to thousands of Pilgrims in St. Peter's Square. (Photo on page 107 by CPP/Osservatore Romano)

Page 108–109: Cardinal Joseph Ratzinger blesses the casket of Pope John Paul II as cardinals look on, during his funeral in St. Peter's Square at the Vatican, Friday, April 8, 2005. Tens of thousands of people jammed St. Peter's Square to say a final farewell to Pope John Paul II in the presence of kings, queens, presidents and prime ministers for a funeral capping one of the largest religious gatherings of all time.

FUNERAL MASS OF POPE JOHN PAUL II

HOMILY

BY JOSEPH CARDINAL RATZINGER

Saint Peter's Square
Friday, April 8, 2005

"Follow me." The Risen Lord says these words to Peter. They are his last words to this disciple, chosen to shepherd his flock. "Follow me"—this lapidary saying of Christ can be taken as the key to understanding the message that comes to us from the life of our late beloved Pope John Paul II. Today we bury his remains in the earth as a seed of immortality—our hearts are full of sadness yet, at the same time, of joyful hope and profound gratitude.

These are the sentiments that inspire us, Brothers and Sisters in Christ, present here in Saint Peter's Square, in neighboring streets, and in various other locations within the city of Rome, where an immense crowd, silently praying, has gathered over the last few days. I greet all of you from my heart. In the name of the College of Cardinals, I also wish to express my respects to Heads of State, Heads of Government and the delegations from various countries. I greet the authorities and official representatives of other Churches and Christian Communities and, likewise, those of different religions. Next I greet the Archbishops, Bishops, priests, religious men and women, and the faithful who have come here from every continent; especially the young, whom John Paul II liked to call the future and the hope

111

of the Church. My greeting is extended, moreover, to all those throughout the world who are united with us through radio and television in this solemn celebration of our beloved Holy Father's funeral.

Follow me—as a young student Karol Wojtyła was thrilled by literature, the theater, and poetry. Working in a chemical plant, surrounded and threatened by the Nazi terror, he heard the voice of the Lord: Follow me! In this extraordinary setting he began to read books of philosophy and theology and then entered the clandestine seminary established by Cardinal Sapieha. After the war he was able to complete his studies in the faculty of theology of the Jagellonian University of Kraków. How often, in his letters to priests and in his autobiographical books, has he spoken to us about his priesthood, to which he was ordained on November 1, 1946. In these texts he interprets his priesthood with particular reference to three sayings of the Lord. First: "You did not choose me, but I chose you. And I appointed you to go and bear fruit, fruit that will last" (Jn 15:16). The second saying is: "The good shepherd lays down his life for the sheep" (Jn 10:11). And then: "As the Father has loved me, so I have loved you; abide in my love" (Jn 15:9). In these three sayings we see the heart and soul of our Holy Father. He really went everywhere, untiringly, in order to bear fruit, fruit that lasts. *Rise, Let Us Be on Our Way!* is the title of his next-to-last book. "Rise, let us be on our way!"—with these words he roused us from a lethargic faith, from the sleep of the disciples of both yesterday and today. "Rise, let us be on our way!" he continues to say to us even today. The Holy Father was a priest to the last, for he offered his life to God for his flock and for the entire human family, in a daily self-oblation for the service of the Church, especially amid the sufferings of his final months. And in this way he became one with Christ, the Good Shepherd who loves his sheep. Finally, "abide in my love": the Pope who tried to meet everyone, who had an ability to forgive and to open his heart to all, tells us once again today, with these words of the Lord, that by abiding in the love of Christ we learn, at the school of Christ, the art of true love.

Follow me! In July 1958 the young priest Karol Wojtyła began a new stage in his journey with the Lord and in the footsteps of the Lord. Karol had gone to the Masuri lakes for his usual vacation, along with a group of young people who loved canoeing. But he brought with him a letter inviting him to call on the Primate of Poland, Cardinal Wyszyński. He could guess the purpose of the meeting: he was to be appointed as the Auxiliary Bishop of Kraków. Leaving the academic world, leaving this challenging engagement with young people, leaving the great intellectual endeavor of striving to understand and interpret the mystery of that creature which is man and of communicating to today's world the Christian interpretation of our being—all this must have seemed to him like losing his very self, losing what had become the very human identity of this young priest. Follow me—Karol Wojtyła accepted the appointment, for he heard in the Church's call the voice of Christ. And then he realized how true are the Lord's words: "Those who try to make their life secure will lose it, but those who lose their life will keep it" (Lk 17:33). Our Pope—and we all know this—never wanted to make his own life secure, to keep it for himself; he wanted to give of himself unreservedly, to the very last moment, for Christ and thus also for us. And thus he came to experience how everything he had given over into the Lord's hands came back to him in a new way. His love of words, of poetry, of literature, became an essential part of his pastoral mission and gave new vitality, new urgency, new attractiveness to the preaching of the gospel, even when it is a sign of contradiction.

Follow me! In October 1978 Cardinal Wojtyła once again heard the voice of the Lord. Once more there took place that dialogue with Peter reported in the Gospel of this Mass: "Simon, son of John, do you love me? Feed my sheep!" To the Lord's question, "Karol, do you love me?" the Archbishop of Kraków answered from the depths of his heart: "Lord you know everything; you know that I love you." The love of Christ was the dominant force in the life of our beloved Holy Father. Anyone who ever saw him pray, who ever heard him preach, knows that. Thanks to his being profoundly rooted in Christ, he was able to bear a burden that transcends merely human abilities: that of being the shepherd of Christ's flock, his universal Church. This is not the time to speak of the specific content of this rich pontificate. I would like only to read two passages of today's liturgy that reflect central elements of his message. In the first reading, Saint Peter says—and with Saint Peter, the Pope himself—"I truly understand that God shows no partiality, but in every nation anyone who fears him and does what is right is acceptable to him. You know the message he sent to the people of Israel, preaching peace by Jesus Christ—he is Lord of all" (Acts 10:34–36). And in the second reading, Saint Paul—and with Saint Paul, our late Pope—exhorts us, crying out: "My brothers and sisters, whom I love and long for, my joy and my crown, stand firm in the Lord in this way, my beloved" (Phil 4:1).

Follow me! Together with the command to feed his flock, Christ proclaimed to Peter that he would die a martyr's death. With those words, which conclude and sum up the dialogue on love and on the mandate of the universal shepherd, the Lord recalls another dialogue, which took place during the Last Supper. There Jesus had said: "Where I am going, you cannot come." Peter said to him, "Lord, where are you going?" Jesus replied: "Where I am going, you cannot follow me now; but you will follow me afterward" (Jn 13:33, 36). Jesus from the Supper went toward the Cross, went toward his Resurrection—he entered into the Paschal Mystery; and Peter could not yet follow him. Now—after the Resurrection—comes the time, comes this "afterward". By shepherding the flock of Christ, Peter enters into the Paschal Mystery, he goes toward the Cross and the Resurrection. The Lord says this in these words: "When you were younger, you used to fasten your own belt and to go wherever you wished. But when you grow old, you will stretch out your hands, and someone else will fasten a belt around you and take you where you do not wish to go" (Jn 21:18). In the first years of his pontificate, still young and full of energy, the Holy Father went to the very ends of the earth, guided by Christ. But afterward, he increasingly entered into the communion of Christ's sufferings; increasingly he understood the truth of the words: "Someone else will fasten a belt around you." And in this very communion with the suffering Lord, tirelessly and with renewed intensity, he proclaimed the gospel, the mystery of that love which goes to the end (cf. Jn 13:1).

He interpreted for us the Paschal Mystery as a mystery of divine mercy. In his last book, he wrote: The limit imposed upon evil "is ultimately Divine Mercy" (*Memory and Identity*, p. 55). And reflecting on the assassination attempt, he said: "In sacrificing himself for us all, Christ gave a new meaning to suffering, opening up a new dimension, a new order: the order of love.... It is this suffering which burns and consumes evil with the flame of love and draws forth even from sin a great flowering of good" (p. 167). Impelled by this vision, the Pope suffered and loved in communion with Christ, and that is why the message of his suffering and his silence proved so eloquent and so fruitful.

Divine Mercy: the Holy Father found the purest reflection of God's mercy in the Mother of God. He, who at an early age had lost his own mother, loved his divine Mother all the more. He heard the words of the crucified Lord as addressed personally to him: "Behold your Mother." And so he did as the beloved disciple did: he took her into his own home (*eis ta idia*: Jn 19:27)—*Totus tuus*. And from the Mother he learned to conform himself to Christ.

None of us can ever forget how in that last Easter Sunday of his life, the Holy Father, marked by suffering, came once more to the window of the Apostolic Palace and one last time gave his blessing *urbi et orbi*. We can be sure that our beloved Pope is standing today at the window of the Father's house, that he sees us and blesses us. Yes, bless us, Holy Father. We entrust your dear soul to the Mother of God, your Mother, who guided you each day and who will guide you now to the eternal glory of her Son, our Lord Jesus Christ. Amen.